W9-CYB-183

TO:_____

FROM:_____

Design by Anderson Thomas Design

Published by C.R. Gibson®
C.R. Gibson® is a registered trademark of Thomas Nelson, Inc.
Nashville, Tennessee 37214

Printed in Mexico.

ISBN 0-7667-6652-7
GB646R

Thank You For Being You

photographs by
KIM ANDERSON

poetry by
PAULA FINN

One of the greatest gifts

of our relationship is the comfort of knowing

I can always be myself with you,

and you will accept me for being just that.

With you,

I never have to laugh when I feel like crying,

or be quiet when I need to talk,

or stay calm when I feel like getting upset,

or sound positive when I need to complain.

The greatest comfort is the knowledge

that when I need a friend...

I NEVER HAVE TO BE ALONE.

I never have to be alone.

IN SHARING OUR FEARS,
we become bolder.

In sharing our losses, we become richer.

In sharing our mistakes, we become wiser.

In sharing ourselves, we become closer.

Our lives were meant to be shared.

IT'S SO COMFORTING TO SHARE
the events of my day with you –

the little things I know you'll find funny, or touching,

or interesting, only because they happened to me.

You know when I need your help or advice,

and when I just need to know that you care.

It's not often that we feel safe

enough with another person to shed our defenses,

and to risk being completely ourselves –

to show them they are important in our life, and that

we would be so much less without them.

I NEED YOU. . .

and I trust you enough to tell you.

You listen to me

without judging,

you support me

without pressuring,

you appreciate me as I am

without comparing

me to what I am not.

You encourage me

in my goals and dreams,

and validate my struggles

to fulfill them...

You are so easy to talk to,

so easy to feel close to, and so easy to love.

YOUR SUPPORT

has deepened my self-confidence,

your humor has brightened my outlook,

and your encouragement has brought me

closer than ever to my dreams.

Always, you've been there to listen, to understand . . .

and to help me grow.

YOUR SUPPORT ADDS
so much to my life.

You share my joy as if it were your own.

You feel my pain and you cry with me.

Thank you for understanding me,

accepting me, and loving me as I am.

IT SOUNDS SIMPLE
but it means so much to say –

I feel comfortable with you.

I don't have to worry about how I look to you

or sound to you or what you're

going to think about me when I'm not around.

I don't have to rehearse or analyze our conversations –

WHEN WE TALK I CAN RELAX.
when we talk I can relax.

I feel comfortable with you. It sounds so simple . . .

BUT IT MEANS SO MUCH.
but it means so much.

You know when I want to be serious;

you know when I need to be playful.

When I'm with you

I am free to express my true mood.

If I'm not feeling happy, or positive, or energetic,

I don't have to act or pretend that I am.

You support my goals, while accepting my faults.

You love the person I am.

Your accepting nature has helped me
to treat others and myself, more gently.

You concentrate on my good points while overlooking
my flaws, and you can always find something in me to praise.

You are so thoughtful.

You give me much more than is

e x p e c t e d

and you expect much less than you

d e s e r v e .

You are strong enough

to admit your weaknesses,

brave enough to express your fears;

free enough to laugh

and human enough to cry.

My life is enriched in so

many ways by your presence,

for in you I have found the friend

I've always wanted...

and the love I'll always need.

TOGETHER

we've laughed and cried,

shared sunshine and storms . . .

we've celebrated carefree days,

and helped each other through

the long troubled nights.

With you life is exciting. With you I can be myself.

With you I feel appreciated. With you I have fun.

With you I am happier than I have ever been.

Thank you for being you.

Your support has made my triumphs more meaningful,

and my losses easier to bear.

I will praise you when you win,

and share your pain if you lose...

A l w a y s, I will accept
you for who you are and not
for how much or how little you achieve.

I will strive to bring out the best in you
while forgiving your faults.

I won't expect perfection
in either of us.

In the tomorrows we share, I pray that I can be

sensitive to your needs, understanding of your concerns,

patient with your mistakes, and comforting of your pain . . .

that I can give as much of myself as you need . . .

and all the love that you deserve.